PACKARD MOTOR CARS
1946 THROUGH 1958
PHOTO ARCHIVE

PACKARD MOTOR CARS 1946 THROUGH 1958
PHOTO ARCHIVE

Photographs from the Detroit Public Library's National Automotive History Collection

Edited with introduction by Mark A. Patrick
Curator, National Automotive History Collection

Iconografix
Photo Archive Series

Iconografix
PO Box 609
Osceola, Wisconsin 54020 USA

Text Copyright © 1996 by Iconografix

Library of Congress Card Number 95-82099

ISBN 1-882256-45-X

96 97 98 99 00 5 4 3 2 1

Cover and book design by Lou Gordon, Osceola, Wisconsin

Printed in the United States of America

Book trade distribution by Voyageur Press, Inc. (800) 888-9653

PREFACE

The histories of machines and mechanical gadgets are contained in the books, journals, correspondence and personal papers stored in libraries and archives throughout the world. Written in tens of languages, covering thousands of subjects, the stories are recorded in millions of words.

Words are powerful. Yet, the impact of a single image, a photograph or an illustration, often relates more than dozens of pages of text. Fortunately, many of the libraries and archives that house the words also preserve the images.

In the *Photo Archive Series,* Iconografix reproduces photographs and illustrations selected from public and private collections. The images are chosen to tell a story-to capture the character of their subject. Reproduced as found, they are accompanied by the captions made available by the archive.

The Iconografix *Photo Archive Series* is dedicated to young and old alike, the enthusiast, the collector and anyone who, like us, is fascinated by "things" mechanical.

Twenty-Third Series Custom Eight Convertible Victoria Model 2333-5 at the 1950 Chicago Auto Show.

INTRODUCTION

The photographs in this book celebrate Packard motor cars manufactured after the Second World War. Commentary on this period too often reads like an epitaph. Some analysis straddles the realm of hypercriticism. Although Packard executives did make some decisions that in some respect turned out to damage the company, to this writer, the relevant and enduring truth is that postwar Packards are wonderful automobiles! Having said that, however, there remain both myths and truths to ponder.

There is an oral tradition that lends a marvelous aura of mystery to the atmosphere of Packard's postwar operations. Perhaps the most intriguing, persistent, yet wholly unfounded of these yarns, is that Communist sympathizers in the Roosevelt administration forced Packard to transfer its prewar body dies to Stalin. Stalin, a Packard enthusiast, wanted the dies to build a Soviet Packard, the ZIS. In actuality, the dies were recycled into scrap metal for the war effort. The ZIS was just a cheap knock-off of a Packard. Even if the yarn was true, the dies were of prewar vintage. Their transfer to Russia would have had no bearing on Packard's performance after the war, as this colorful tale would seem to imply.

Another belief is that the government deliberately denied the "elitist" Packard Motor Car Company lucrative defense contracts. Such awards would have bolstered the balance sheet and provided the needed capital to create new styles and introduce new technologies. While there may be some merit in this suggestion, it is overstated—Packard did have government contracts, to an extent that other enterprises found the company attractive as an investment.

To many of the discriminating public in the postwar years, especially those of means, there was a perception that Packard was outmoded. Admittedly, Packard was late to recognize some important changes in public taste. Consider that Packard stayed with the in-line eight cylinder engine through 1954. Though an outstanding and proven engine, the public had come to regard the V-8 engine as the industry standard. Packard did introduce a V-8 in 1955, but too late to make the impact on public perceptions that was needed. The company might also have been criticized for a certain reluctance to offer more modern styling features. As Packard did too little to change such public perceptions, when certain models did have verve and joie de vivre, the public was jaded.

What is remarkable is that Packard, by the early Fifties a small player in the automobile industry, was actually an industry leader in some areas. The Packard Ultramatic transmission, introduced in late 1949, was recognized as one of the best automatic transmissions available. The Packard Tortion-level suspension, introduced in 1955, eliminated springs and added a motor that controlled torsion bars that automatically leveled the vehicle, regardless of road conditions.

Much of Packard's misfortune can, doubtlessly, be laid at the feet of its management. Packard not only lagged somewhat in training a new generation of leadership, it also created a milieu in which qualified employees jumped ship. In 1954, the beginning of the end, Packard bought Studebaker. The move was part of a strategy to create an alliance of smaller manufacturers that might better compete in the volatile automotive market. The strategy failed, as there was not enough capital for further mergers. In any case, the spirit was gone by the mid-Fifties. Studebaker-Packard Corporation itself became vulnerable to a takeover, and that is just what occurred. In 1956, it was purchased by Curtiss-Wright Corporation, who stripped the company of its government contracts. Studebaker-Packard dropped the Packard line in 1958 and Studebaker limped along to the mid-Sixties. Packard, one of the greatest of all the motor companies did not go down in glorious flames of Götterdämmerung, but rather in a lousy, paltry business deal.

These photographs show the evolution of Packard from 1946 through 1958. The 1946 and 1947 Packards were essentially prewar Clippers—graceful, but not new. Packard dropped the six cylinder after 1947 and struck with the straight eight until 1955. The all new Packards were the Standard, Deluxe, Super, and Custom Eights. In 1951, Packard introduced the Twenty-Fourth Series. These were more modern in appearance and are distinguished by what another writer, Michael Scott, called the "it crawled from the sea" grille. Actually, this grille is peculiar—its effect is dramatic and attractive on convertible models, but rather atrocious on coupes and sedans. Another striking feature to look for is the rear quarter panel series of jet louvers.

Nineteen Fifty-Five brought major changes in Packard models. As a group, they are glorious automobiles— some of the finest of the decade, with delightful, expressive two and three-tone finishes and horizontal grille lines. A particularly interesting feature of the 1955 models was the rear design. Carried over from 1954, its understated appearance provided a nice balance to the angles of the hood and grille.

In 1957, all production of Packards was transferred to

South Bend, Indiana. For 1957 and 1958 models, Dick Teague, the great stylist, added some trim features which distinguished Packards from Studebakers. Alas! At their foundation, the last Packards were Studebakers.

The photographs appearing in *Packard Motor Cars 1946 through 1958 Photo Archive* are from the Detroit Public Library's National Automotive History Collection. We are nearly 50 years old. The mission of the NAHC is to retain and preserve the historical record of the automobile and other forms of wheeled transportation. Toward this aim, the NAHC has become the premier collection of its type. Our files include 350,000 pieces of sales literature and 250,000 photographs. The collection also houses biographical files, books, magazines, art blueprints, owner's manuals, and personal papers of automotive pioneers and trailblazers. Much of this material is unique. Most importantly, it is in the public library and, therefore, is accessible to the enthusiast.

1946 - 1947

Twenty-First Series

Photographed and identified in June 1945 as a Twenty-First Series Model 180. Once in production, it was designated the Custom Super Clipper.

Left and front views of the Model 2106 Custom Super Clipper Touring Sedan. Again, these are probably pre-production automobiles.

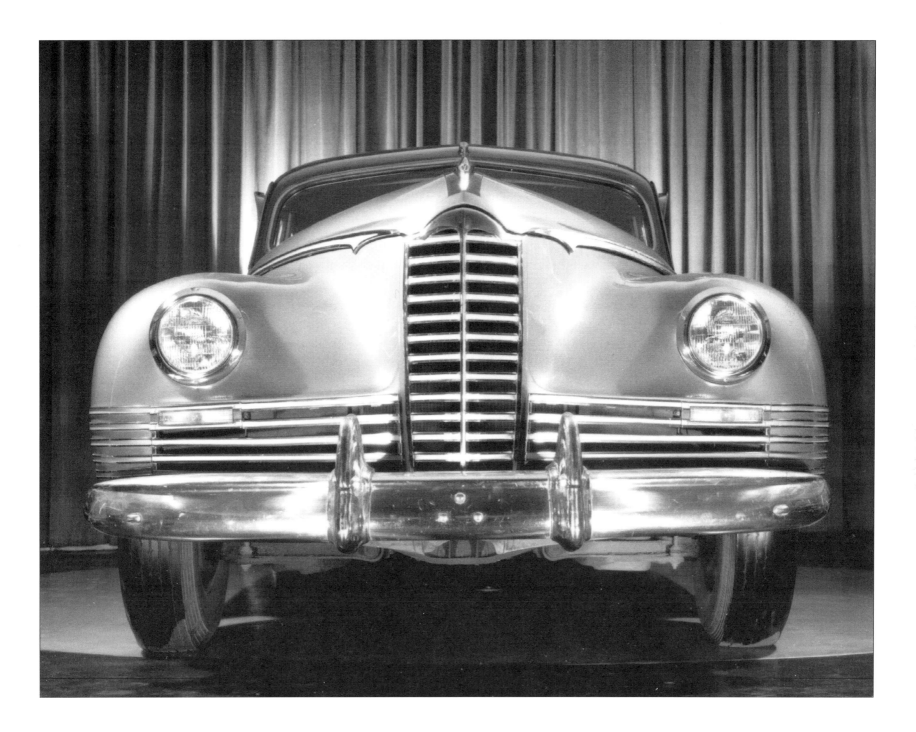

1946 Model 2101 Standard Clipper Eight Sedan.

Model 2103 Super Clipper Four-Door Sedan.

Two views of Model 2103 Super Clipper Club Sedans.

Model 2111 Deluxe Clipper Club Sedans in single and two-tone paint schemes.

Model 2111 Deluxe Clipper Four Door Sedan.

Model 2126 Custom Super Clipper Limousine.

Twenty-First Series Custom Eight Limousine Hearse by Henney.

Two views of Model 2126 Custom Super Clipper Seven-Passenger Sedans.

Identified as a 1947 Custom Super Eight, this appears to be a modified Custom Super Clipper Seven-Passenger Sedan.

1948 - 1949

Twenty-Second Series

A retouched photograph of a Twentieth Series Clipper illustrating a proposal for front grille treatment, as applied to the Twenty-Second Series.

A production prototype of the Twenty-Second Series Packard.

Model 2201 Standard Eight Four-Door Sedan.

Model 2202 Super Eight Four-Door Sedan.

30

Model 2202 Super Eight Club Sedan.

Model 2202 Eight Club Sedan.

Interior view of the Model 2206 Custom Eight Touring Sedan.

Two views of Model 2201 Standard Eight Station Sedans.

Rear and interior views of the 2201 Standard Eight Station Sedan.

Model 2232 Super Eight Convertible Victoria show car.

Model 2232 Super Eight Convertible Victoria.

Model 2233 Custom Eight Convertible Victoria, the choice of 1948 US Presidential candidates. Above, Mr. and Mrs. Thomas E. Dewey. Opposite, President Harry S Truman.

1948 Custom Eight Convertible Victoria in Oslo, Norway.

Model 2226 Custom Eight Long Wheelbase Seven-Passenger Sedan by Henney.

The Henney-Packard stand at the 1948 National Funeral Directors Association convention. Left front, Model 2226 Custom Eight Seven-Passenger Sedan; left, behind sedan, Model 2213 Custom Eight Limousine Ambulance; center, Model 2213 Custom Eight Landau Three-Way Hearse; beyond center, at right, Model 2213 Custom Eight Limousine Ambulance; far right, Model 2213 Custom Eight Limousine Flower Car.

More than 25 Model 2213 Custom Eight Limousine Flower Cars operated by a single New York funeral home.

Packard Six, Model 2220 New York-type (long wheelbase) Taxi.

Packard Six, Model 2240 Sedan Taxi.

A lineup of 10 Packard Six, Model 2240 Sedan Taxis.

1949-1950

Twenty-Third Series

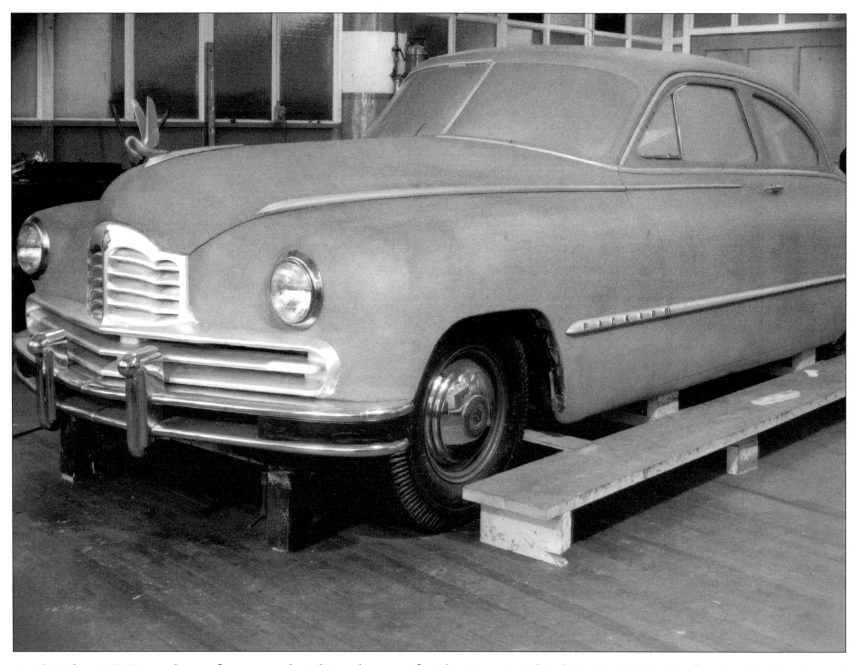

An October 1947 mockup of proposed styling changes for the Twenty-Third Series. Note the front grille treatment that did not survive, and the side body chrome strip that did, but in a revised form and placed in a higher position.

Note the rear bumper and taillight treatment, and the longer side body chrome strip.

At left, 1949 Model 2306 Custom Eight Touring Sedan. At right, 1949 Model 2333 Custom Eight Covertible Victoria.

54

1949 Model 2302 Super Deluxe Four-Door Sedan.

1949 Model 2302 Super Eight Four-Door Sedan.

1949 Model 2301 Eight Club Sedan.

1949 Model 2301 Eight Station Sedan.

1949 Model 2333 Custom Eight
Covertible Victoria.

1950 Model 2332-5 Super Eight
Convertible Victoria.

1950 Model 2302-5 Super Eight Deluxe Touring Sedan.

1951 and 1952
Twenty-Fourth and Twenty-Fifth Series

1951 Chicago Auto Show display.

1951 models on the proving grounds. Front to back: 400 Model 2406, 300 Model 2402, and 200 Model 2401.

1951 300 Model 2402 Four-Door Sedan.

1951 400 Model 2406 Patrician Sedan.

1951 250 Model 2431 Convertible.

1951 250 Model 2431 Mayfair Sports Hardtop, companion to the 250 Convertible.

Phantom II Speedster, as built for Mr. Edward Macauley in the Packard Motor Car Company shops. A modified 1952 Model 2501 Deluxe Club Sedan.

The Packard Pan American, the 1952 show car. Designed by Richard Arib and built by Henney, it was arguably the most stylish car of its day.

1952 300 Model 2502 Four-Door Sedan.

1952 400 Model 2506 Patrician Sedan.

1952 400 Model 2506 Patrician Sedan. The car in this photograph of November 1951 featured "fashion-keyed" two-tone hues selected by "world famed color stylist and decorator, Dorothy Draper."

250 Model 2531 Mayfair Sport Coupe.

Two views of 250 Model 2531 Convertibles.

1953 Twenty-Sixth Series

The Packard Balboa, the 1953 show car based on the 2631 Caribbean. Design work by Richard Teague. The two photographs reveal trim differences at the windows and on the spare tire cover.

Model 2606 Patrician Sedan, formerly the Four Hundred.

An early Model 2631 Convertible with rear fender louvers, dropped in later production.

Two views of Model 2631 Caribbean Convertibles. Actors Tony Curtis, Janet Leigh, and Don Taylor grace the automobile above.

Two views of the Model 2626 Seven-Passenger Sedan by Henney.

Model 2606 Formal Sedan by Derham.

1954 Fifty-Fourth Series

The 1954 Packard lineup displayed at the entrance to the proving grounds.

The fiberglass-bodied Packard Panther Daytona, the 1954 show car, displayed at the New York International Auto Show. Design work by Richard Teague.

Two views of the Model 5400 Clipper
Special Two-Door Sedan.

Model 5401 Clipper Deluxe Four-Door Sedan.

Model 5401 Clipper Deluxe Club Sedan.

Model 5401 Clipper Sportster Two-Door Sedan. This was a show car, with painted grille surround and Panama script on rear fender.

Two views of a Model 5402 Cavalier Four-Door Sedan.

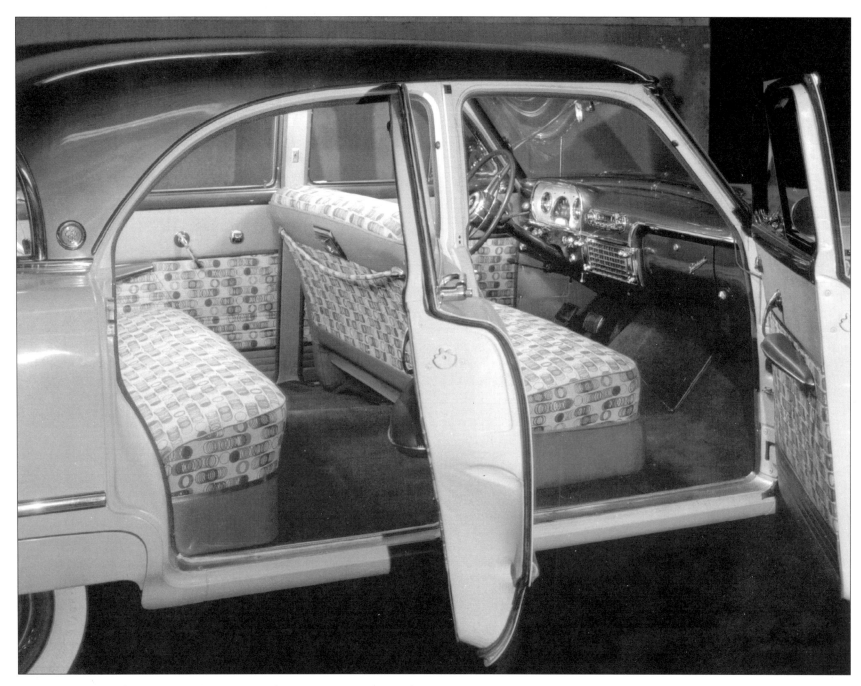

The interior of a Model 5402 Cavalier Four-Door Sedan.

The interior of a Model 5431 Pacific Hardtop.

Model 5411 Clipper Super Panama Hardtop.

Model 5411 Clipper Special Four-Door Sedan.

Model 5431 Convertible.

Model 5431 Caribbean Convertible.

Model 5426 Patrician Limousine by Henney.

1955 Fifty-Fifth Series

The Packard Request, the 1955 show car based on a Model 5580 Four Hundred Hardtop with Caribbean side styling. Design work by Richard Teague.

Experimental Model 5580 Patrician Four-Door Sedan. This car participated in an endurance run certified by the American Automobile Association. Between October 21 and 31, 1954, the car was driven 25,000 miles on the proving ground track in Utica, Michigan. Total elapsed time was 238 hours, 41 minutes, 44.3 seconds.

Two views of Model 5560 Clipper Custom Constellations.

Model 5580 Patrician Four-Door Sedan.

Model 5560 Custom Clipper Sedan.

Model 5580 Caribbean Convertible sporting one of four optional three-tone paint schemes.

1956 Fifty-Sixth Series

The Packard Predictor, the 1956 show car, displayed at the 1956 Chicago Auto Show. Design work by Richard Teague.

An Atlantic City salon showing of the 1956 Packard lineup.

Model 5640 Clipper Super Panama Hardtop.

Model 5640 Clipper Deluxe Four-Door Sedan.

Model 5660 Clipper Custom Four-Door Sedan.

Model 5670 Executive Four-Door Sedan.

Model 5680 Patrician Four-Door Sedan.

Model 5688 Caribbean Convertible.

Two views of Model 5680 Four Hundred Hardtops.

1957 and 1958

Fifty-Seventh and Fifty-Eighth Series

Two views of the 1957 Model 57L
Clipper Town Sedan.

1957 Model 57L Clipper Country Sedan.

The optional rear-facing third seat, as available on the Clipper Country Sedan.

1958 Model 58L Hardtop.

1958 Model 58L Country Sedan.

1958 Model 58L Hawk Hardtop.

The Iconografix Photo Archive Series includes:

AUTOMOTIVE

AMERICAN SERVICE STATIONS 1935-1943 Photo Archive	ISBN 1-882256-27-1
IMPERIAL 1955-1963 Photo Archive	ISBN 1-882256-22-0
IMPERIAL 1964-1968 Photo Archive	ISBN 1-882256-23-9
LE MANS 1950: THE BRIGGS CUNNINGHAM CAMPAIGN Photo Archive	ISBN 1-882256-21-2
PACKARD 1935-1942 Photo Archive	ISBN 1-882256-44-1
PACKARD 1946-1958 Photo Archive	ISBN 1-882256-45-X
PHILLIPS 66 1945-1954 Photo Archive	ISBN 1-882256-42-5
SEBRING 12-HOUR RACE 1970 Photo Archive	ISBN 1-882256-20-4
STUDEBAKER 1933-1942 Photo Archive	ISBN 1-882256-24-7
STUDEBAKER 1946-1958 Photo Archive	ISBN 1-882256-25-5

TRUCKS

DODGE TRUCKS 1929-1947 Photo Archive	ISBN 1-882256-36-0
DODGE TRUCKS 1948-1960 Photo Archive	ISBN 1-882256-37-9
STUDEBAKER TRUCKS 1927-1940 Photo Archive	ISBN 1-882256-40-9
STUDEBAKER TRUCKS 1941-1964 Photo Archive	ISBN 1-882256-41-7

AVAILABLE EARLY 1996

COCA-COLA: A HISTORY IN PHOTOGRAPHS 1930-1969	ISBN 1-882256-46-8
COCA-COLA: ITS VEHICLES IN PHOTOGRAPHS 1930-1969	ISBN 1-882256-00-X

The Iconografix Photo Archive Series is available from direct mail specialty book dealers and bookstores worldwide, or can be ordered from the publisher. For additional information or to add your name to our mailing list contact:

Iconografix
PO Box 609
Osceola, Wisconsin 54020 USA

Telephone: (715) 294-2792
(800) 289-3504
Fax: (715) 294-3414

Book trade distribution by Voyageur Press, Inc., PO Box 338, Stillwater, Minnesota 55082 USA (800) 888-9653

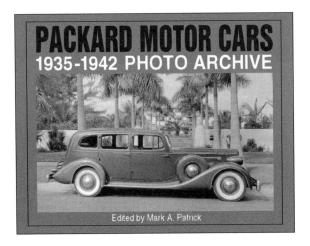
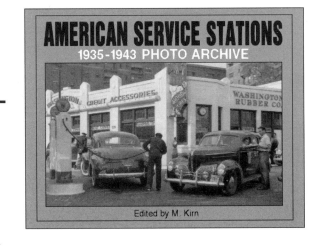
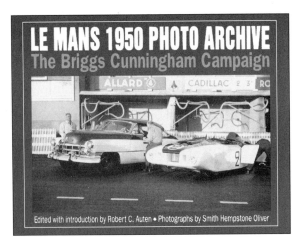
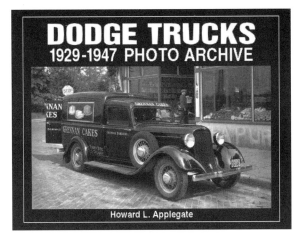
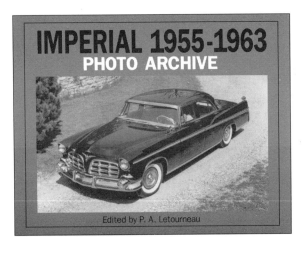

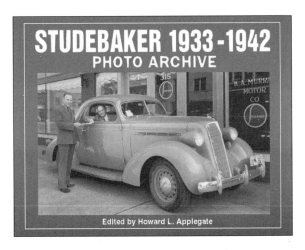